When You Really
Embarrass Yourself
Nobody Ever Forgets

For Caroline,
whose stories are
better!

Stephen Willoughby

When You Really Embarrass Yourself Nobody Ever Forgets

by

Stephen Douglas Williford

THE LINCOLN-BRADLEY PUBLISHING GROUP

Permissions Department
The Lincoln-Bradley Publishing Group
P.O. Box 808
Gatlinburg, TN 37738

Editor: Carl Mays
Project Coordinator: Sharon Theobald
Cover Photograph: Jay Shappley
Cover Design: Eric Robinette
Interior Design and Make-up: Electronic Publishing Services, Inc.

Publisher's Cataloging and Publication
(Prepared by *Quality Books, Inc.*)

Williford, Stephen Douglas.
    When you really embarrass yourself nobody ever forgets /
Stephen Douglas Williford.
    p. cm.
    ISBN 1-879111-06-3

1. American wit and humor 2. Embarrassment—I. Title

PN6162.W55 1994   818'.5402

                                        QBI94-554

When You Really Embarrass Yourself Nobody Ever Forgets

Like other successful books, I wanted mine to have glowing testimonials from several well-known celebrities. I share with you now some of the responses I received to my invitation to review my manuscript.

Don't send the manuscript.

Tom Brokaw

I'm sorry, but I've been swamped with blurb requests, and I'm all blurbed out.

Dave Barry, _Owner, Two Dogs_

Mr. Redford is honored that you would think of him to review your book. Unfortunately, he does not have time to read your letter.

Assistant to **Robert Redford**

Don't send your manuscript to Mr. Cosby, but does he still get the Elvis pen you offered?

Assistant to **Bill Cosby**

I'll never forget the day my father and I hosted the Father-Son Breakfast at church. He never will either because just before he was to speak, I spilled my cup of coffee in his lap.

Steve Williford

Story Locations

Introduction

Can you remember when you were *really* embarrassed? I bet you can remember the time, the place and even who was there. The reason that you can remember who was there is that through the years, they keep reminding you of that embarrassing moment.

It's a universal axiom:

> *When you **really** embarrass yourself*
> *nobody **ever** forgets.*

The first basketball game of my Senior year in high school is a good case in point. I was so excited that the coach chose me to lead the team out of the locker room that I didn't notice the sign the cheerleaders were holding. The cheerleaders were so excited that they didn't notice they weren't holding the sign at ground level - more like ankle height. The sign's structural wire served as a trip wire. It caused me to soar through the gymnasium air, land on the basketball which knocked every cubic inch of air out of my body, and create a laughing frenzy, leaving the fans so weak, they could barely point. Let me just say this about that embarrassing moment. They didn't forget.

I'm sure that your friends and loved ones haven't forgotten your embarrasing moments either. At the time, some well-meaning person, in an attempt to comfort you, no doubt said, "Don't worry, in a few years, everyone will forget."

That well-meaning person lied to you.
They never forget.

Added Benefit!

As a discriminating reader and wise investor, you will recognize this book to be a *collector's item*. This is a *first edition*. This book will not only *provide hours of unrestrained guffawing*, but it will also prove to be a *wise investment* in the years to come. Readers in future generations will think, **What unrestrained guffawing I'm having . . . for hours! I only wish I'd bought a first edition.**

Don't let this happen to you.

Buy This Book and Become Family!

Let me ask you, what satisfaction do you *really* get out of buying a book by Dave Barry, Jerry Seinfeld, Erma Bombeck or Patrick McManus? Oh, sure you'll laugh . . . a lot. But you're only a measly one out of *millions* of readers. Let's face it, they'll never even *know* you bought their books. You deserve more appreciation.

But when you buy *my* book, I'll *know*. I'll come over to your house and bring pizza. We'll roast some marshmellows and make hot chocolate and I'll listen to *your* stories! Plus, your purchase will **significantly** affect the sales of my book, so you will actually get far more for your money. If you'll dim the lights, I'd like to illustrate this with a slide:

When you buy a book by Dave, Jerry, Erma or Pat, the pitiful impact you make is:

But when you buy **this** book, your impact will be like this:

Plus in years to come, people will say, "What's that book?"

If you say, "It's Dave Barry's," they'll say, "Oh,"
because they see them everywhere.

But if you say, "It's Steve Williford's," they'll say, **Let me see that! This is really rare. A first edition! I'll give you $100 for it right here, right now!**

By the Way . . .

Each embarrassing story that I share with you is true. In an attempt to prevent embarrassment or retaliation, many of the names have been changed to Bob.

The View From The Top Had A Straw In It

There are moments in life you never forget.

I had flown up to look at the galleys of my book, *The Longaberger Story*, profiling the amazing career of multi-hundred millionaire entrepreneur Dave Longaberger. Dave, the publisher and I went out to eat one night in a popular, but dimly lit, eating spot.

As we were sitting there, the thought occurred to me,

This is what all the hard work is about. Here I am, sitting across from Dave Longaberger and the book's publisher. This is GREAT! I reached for my glass.

Now in case you don't remember, this was a dimly lit eating establishment. It's hard to see things in a dark restaurant

like your food, or

the person across the table, or

. . . those *little* red straws they put in the glasses.

I lifted the glass and - how can I put this delicately - the straw reached my face before the glass did, and, well, the sucker rammed right up my nose.

I am now sitting across from these two accomplished individuals - with a straw up my nose.

As I held the glass in front of my face, I had to ask myself, *What do I do now?* They don't prepare you for this crisis in college. ("Class, our topic in Etiquette Catastrophies 101 is What to do if You Accidentally Stick a Straw up Your Nose in Public.") I wanted to be as graceful and inconspicuous as possible. Yet, I also wanted the red harpoon out of my nostril.

I quickly arrived upon a plan. "Maybe if I nonchalantly put the glass down, they won't notice. After all, it *is* dark in here." I executed my plan to perfection. I don't think they suspected a thing. And they probably never would have **IF THE STRAW HAD GONE WITH THE GLASS.**

Upon inspection, I noticed there was no straw in the glass. I felt around the vicinity of my nose and ascertained the straw was still firmly planted. I then fell upon plan B, which was to quickly yank it out and utter that witticism that I always carry around for such occasions -

Ooops!

They looked sympathetically at me for a long moment and the publisher said something like, "You okay? I bet that hurt. That straw was way up there!"

I smiled. They smiled.

Dave finally asked, "You want a new straw?"

What to Do if Your Child

Eats a Stink Bug

When you become a parent, no one gives you a list of scenarios to prepare for. Take stink bugs for example.

One day, our two year old daughter saw a stink bug crawling by her and did what any self-respecting toddler would do -

she ate it.

It happened too quickly for Andrea or me to prevent. I know what you're thinking. Yes, we had a *bug* in the house. It happens. So there we are, not knowing what to do. No one ever sat down with us and said, "I want to tell you exactly what to do in case Brittney ever swallows a stink bug."

We looked at our list of emergency numbers on the refrigerator.

9-1-1? Maybe that's overkill.

Police? No.

Fire Department? No.

Pizza Hut Delivery? No.

Poison Control Hot Line? Close enough.

So we call the Poison Control Hot Line and get,

Poison Control Hotline, Dr. Halfi speaking.

From his accent, it was a safe bet that Dr. Halfi did not grow up in Southaven, Mississippi, or the Western Hemisphere, for that matter.

"Hello Doctor. We're calling because our daughter - well - she just ate a bug."

Ate a bog?

"That's right, and we wanted to call and see if it was dangerous."

Um Hmm. Now, why don't you tell me about this bog. Do you know what kind was it?

"Yes sir. It was a stink bug."

*A **stick** bog?*

"No, a **stink** bog."

Stiiiieeeekkkkk bog? How do you spell it?

"S-t-i-n-k."

*Oh, a **stick** bug.*

". . . right."

Can you tell me anything about it? Why is it called a stick bog?

"Well, it's a bug that emits an odor when it becomes afraid."

Ooooouuuuu! So, I would guess the bog became afraid before ingested.

"That would be my bet. Look, we were just calling to see if we should be concerned."

I see. Okay. Let me do a little research and I call you back.

After a few minutes, Dr. Halfi called back, *Mr Willifood? I have found no indications that the bog emitting the stiking odor is harmful, so I wouldn't worry.*

"Okay, that's good news. Thank you, Doctor."

However, I would recommend that you give your child something to get rid of the stick in her mouth.

How to Humiliate Yourself

In Front of the Home Crowd In Such a Way That They'll Remember It For the Rest of Your Life

After a particularly heart stopping, breath taking, knee buckling, mind numbing, humiliatingly embarrassing moment, some wise person may offer such words of comfort as, "Don't worry about it. A few years from now, no one will ever remember it happened."

That person lied to you.

One of my most embarrassing moments happened in high school, and I hear about it fairly often. As a matter of fact, the first time I was asked to speak at my alma mater's sports banquet, I felt flattered, until I learned it was only so I could recount my unfortunate athletic episode.

We were nervous. It was our first game of the basketball season. Coach Armstrong was giving us his pregame chalk talk. *Men, I don't have to tell you how important this game is. We must establish our team as a serious competitor.*

As Coach talked, we could hear the crowd. We could smell the popcorn. I felt my heart pounding. This was it.

My Senior year. The first game of my Senior year. My first year to play on the varsity. My first year to wear a warm-up less than ten years old.

Coach Armstrong continued, *Hutchison, remember to roll after you set the pick.* This was Coach's first year, too. We could tell he was as excited as we were.

Sullivan, look for the open man. LaVelle, remember, three seconds in the lane. Cunningham, Dahlberg, don't be afraid to take the shot if you're open.

Now when we go out, I want you to do lay ups from the left, then the three man weave and then the star drill.

You notice that so far, Coach hadn't mentioned my name. He rarely did. I didn't start. I mostly sat. There's still a groove on that bench that should have my name on it. That's how I got to be Sports Editor for the school paper. They knew I'd be at the games anyway.

My only controversial article of the entire season dealt with when we played in Mole Hill, Arkansas. The gym's floor was so uneven that if you dribbled within two feet of the out-of-bounds line, the ball ricocheted against the wall. As a matter of fact, I wrote that a player actually fell in a rut on the floor so deep, that if it weren't for a referee's quick thinking and long whistle lanyard, the player might have been lost for the rest of the game.

But I digress.

As Coach talked to us, I saw a sock behind him standing up all by itself. You see sights like that in boys' locker rooms. That baby hadn't seen the inside of a washing machine since our Freshman year.

Let's go out there and show them what we can do! Coach said, producing the season's brand new, right out of the box, bright orange, leather smelling, Wilson basketball. Coach turned to me, shoved the ball in my stomach and said, *Lead the team out, Williford!*

I couldn't believe it. Here it was, our first game of our Senior year and the coach chose *me* to lead the team out.

This kind of luck certainly only happened once in a lifetime.

I ran through the locker room with the rest of the team yelling and screaming behind me. I made the 90 degree turn into the gym and was met by a sea of white . . .

I thought that in my excitement, I'd missed the door and run into the wall. But then, the locker room wall hadn't been white since our Kindergarten year.

The sea of white turned out to be a paper sign that the cheerleaders held for the team to burst through. Since this was also the cheerleaders' first game of the basketball season, they overlooked a very important fundamental in sign holding.

In order for the sign to maintain its circular shape, the cheerleaders first created a circle of wire and attached the paper to it. It's critical to the success of the endeavor for such signs to be flush with the floor.

This one wasn't. More like ankle height.

When I burst through the sign, my ankle hit the wire and I *flew* into the gym, landing abruptly on the ball, which knocked every cubic inch of air out of me.

David LaVelle and Harry Hutchison fell on top of me. The rest of the team ran on top of us. David and Harry jumped up and ran over to the team. I buffered their fall.

I was mortified but I couldn't rejoin the team. I couldn't move. I couldn't breathe. All I could do was look.

I saw cheerleaders laughing so hard they almost dropped the rest of the sign on top of me. Even Lynn Hurley, a cheerleader and the girl of my dreams, helped sabotage me before the home crowd.

I saw the crowd, a thundering sea of red faces, laughing so hard they could barely point.

The guys on the other team were giving each other the 1970's equivalent of high fives.

Coach Armstrong came over and helped me over to the bench. I finally joined the team, just in time for the star drill. They just stared at me.

We beat Byhalia 60-58, but somehow I knew I'd never lead the team out again. I also knew my groove in the bench was going to get a lot deeper.

The Case of the Sun God's Sunburned Feet

I *hate* Florida.

A lot of people *love* Florida. There is a reason for this. They tan. I do not tan. I maintain the approximate skin tone of the Pillsbury Dough Boy.

Redheads usually do not tan.

Freckle, yes.

Burn, yes.

Tan, no.

If you see a redhead with a tan, the odds are the red came out of the same kind of a tube Coppertone does.

When forced by family and friends to leave the well-shaded condo and humiliate my white-skinned self among a herd of tanned people, I am forced to do something else I despise - grease up.

I think any rational human should have an aversion to smearing on your body a substance the same consistency as brake fluid.

I can't win in Florida. If I stay in, my wife and friends accuse me of being a kill-joy, a stick in the mud, a fuddy-duddy, a wet blanket, a dead head, a party pooper.

According to tradition, after about the second day, I usually break from the peer pressure and hit the beach, knowing that I will suffer twice.

First, my loved ones, my dearest friends, have no mercy or hesitancy in public humiliation. Last summer, for example, I cautiously, but cooperatively, entered the pool area. When my tanable friends caught sight of Steve, the good sport, it was, *Oh, look, the Sun God! It's Steve Savage. It's the Great White Shark. The Last of the Coppertones!*

Second, no matter how much I might prepare, I always get sunburned somewhere. And should I point out my pain, the sympathetic response I receive is, "You should have used sun screen there."

I thought last year I had actually covered every cubic inch of my exposed skin. I spent about four weeks applying Sun block #2769 - in *coats*. I wore a big T-shirt and some green, K-Mart, knee-length jams. I took a walk on the beach with my friend, Bob, and our families. We stopped to watch a nearby fishing boat pull in its nets. When we returned, the sunscreen had done it's job - the part that wasn't washed off by water, that is.

I had the reddest feet this side of Red Lobster.

Can you imagine the howls that arose poolside when I made my crimson-footed entrance? I'll have to admit, when I wasn't trying to sleep and when the Solarcaine had been recently applied, it *was* a funny sight. Of course, it would have been even funnier if it had happened to someone else.

I'm looking forward to that day in a few decades when these people's skin looks like something that needs Armor-All. Of course, I'll be pale and washed-out, but come to think of it, that's how I am now. At least I'll have time to work on my lines and they'll have used up all theirs.

"Hey, pass me that football - oh, I'm sorry Bob, it's you." "Nice coat, Andrea. A little warm to be wearing leather, though - oops, my mistake."

But, they'll probably be so old they won't hear me or the people who ask me if they're my parents.

Snow Embarassed
at Crested Butte

My friend Bob was going skiing in Colorado. Crested
Butte. It was his first time - anywhere. There's not a lot
of skiing around Memphis. The closest hill is Bald
Knob, Arkansas, a hundred miles away. There are
only two problems with skiing Bald Knob.

One, the hill is not high enough. It would take about
six seconds to ski it, even with turns.

Two, there is snow for only about a day and a half each
winter.

Bob was excited about his upcoming Colorado ski trip
and approached me for pointers and free ski wear. I
asked what he needed. He answered whatever a skier
needs to wear.

I told Bob that it had been a few years since I had skied,
but he was welcome to anything I had. The **it had
been a few years since I skied** is integral to the story.
Bob said he was sure it would be fine, since it meant he
didn't have to spend any money.

I remember when I bought that ski outfit. It was on sale
at Sears in Memphis about 1977. It was the only ski
outfit in the store, and I think even so, it had been there
since Clinton had a beard. It was a brilliant red with
yellow stripes at the top.

When I gave Bob the outfit, along with various other ski-related articles, he commented, "Wow! Kind of *bright* isn't it?"

I laughed.

He laughed.

Then he went to Crested Butte and was gone for a week.

The next time I saw Bob, I asked how the ski trip went.

I could see from his eyes, he had a message he'd been waiting to communicate.

"Do you know how many people skied Crested Butte each day?"

"No. Thousands, I guess."

"That's right. Over twelve thousand each day."

"Wow."

"Would you like to know how many other of those twelve thousand skiers had on a suit like mine?"

"I wouldn't know."

"Well, I would. Because I looked. None. We skied for five days. That's over 60,000 skiers. Not one wore a suit like mine. Although during the course of each day, most of them had a comment about this one."

"Oh?"

"Including the members of my own group. They never had any trouble finding me."

"Um hmm."

"Now, that would be bad enough if I were a decent skier. But no, I had to wear the one-of-a-kind suit my first year. I didn't fade into the background as just another novice skier. I was the beginner with the fluorescent ski outfit on. People would say, "Look, he fell again. That's the same guy that fell coming off the ski lift.""

Bob has been back several more times, and each year when he returns, he gives me his running tally on how many ski suits he's seen like mine. Which is equal to the same number of items he's subsequently borrowed from me.

The Difference Between
Men and Women

There is one undeniable difference between women and men.

Ask any woman, and she'll have this. As far as medical science can tell, no man has ever had one.

A Kleenex.

You can travel to any part of the world, tap a woman on the shoulder and in any language ask, "Excuse me, but do you have a Kleenex?" She'll rummage around in her purse and eventually pull out a Kleenex. It may have been in there for a couple of presidential terms. It may be rumpled and smell of Wrigley's Spearmint Gum and Chanel Number Five. It may have a piece of gum in it or some make-up on it, but it'll be in there.

Walk up to a man anywhere in the world and ask for a Kleenex. You won't get one. You may get a handkerchief. I wouldn't take it if I were you. In the first place, what if it's been used? In the second place, while a Kleenex has been stored in a purse next to the keys, compact and some tic-tacs, the handkerchief has been in the man's back pocket. . .

When you think about it, a handkerchief is pretty gross. Can you imagine a guy who's never seen a handkerchief before and witnesses it being used for the first time?

"Yeah," he explains to his buddy, "he was about to sneeze and he whips this white cloth out of his back pocket, and, well, he sneezed right into the thing."

"No!" his amazed friend gasps.

"Yeah, but you haven't heard the worst. Then, he puts it back in his *pocket!*"

"Aaaaiiiggghhhh!"

At the next public gathering you attend, ask: "Does anyone have a Kleenex?"

The men: "What?"

The women: "Here."

What do you do if you don't have a Kleenex? Again the difference is defined by sex.

If they can get away with it, men will do the easiest thing. Let's just leave it at that.

The standard recourse for women is to go into the bathroom and fold toilet paper to resemble Kleenex.

But Kleenexes are not the only difference between men and women. As an added bonus, here are a few others:

Bending over. When you have to pick something up from the ground, like a newspaper or a quarter or a Kleenex.

Men will squat. They will bend their knees and resemble a baseball catcher behind the plate, or a weight lifter about to heave.

Women will not bend their knees. They will bend at the waist as if they have no knees. Their head and feet touch each other which means something else is now pointing straight up. If a man attempted this, he would be in traction for three days.

Remote Control. This is the sacred object of a man's castle. It controls a man's domain. Men *must* flip the channels. It's inate. Remote controls were made to be used.

It's simply not enough to watch a PBS documentary. There's the urge to know how the game is going on ESPN, as well as the game on five other stations, as well as the movies on CBS, NBC, HBO and the Movie Channel. But there's also a couple of movie classics, a game show, *Andy Griffith, Matlock, The Munsters, Captain Kangaroo, My Favorite Martian and Bonanza,* all going on simultaneously. Who could leave those treasures untapped? Women.

Communication. I've observed that women like to talk about serious subjects at the exact opposite time that men do, which is never.

The words that men dread above all others from women are,

We need to talk.

Also, for some reason, the time that women want to talk to men is with three seconds left in double overtime of the NCAA championship final game.

If men had our way, we'd never talk about anything more serious than comparing when our mothers threw away our baseball card collections.

I've learned that my wife and I know different facts about our new friends. For example, after I've met someone new, my wife will ask:

How many children does he have?

"I don't know. Maybe two."

Boys or girls?

"I don't know."

I guess you don't know how old they are either.

"No. But I do know that they have a dog."

*What **do** men talk about? You don't know **anything** about him!*

When my wife meets a new friend, I ask:

So what does she do?

"I don't know."

Uh huh. What does her husband do?

"I don't know. I think they have a dog, though"

Directions. When on a trip, there's a big difference between the sexes regarding directions. Women will ask.

Men will, too, four hours later than women. Even if a man has seen nothing which remotely resembles *anything* on the map for 100 miles, he always believes that just over the next hill things will come together.

Eating Habits. Women do not order desserts. They let men order dessert and say, "I'll just have a bite of yours." This is a death knell to the man's dessert.

If four men eat a meal together, they each throw some bills on the table and tell the waiter to keep the change. If four women eat together, they whip out their calculators and figure out exactly, to the penny, how much each person owes and exactly how much the tip should be. And they *always* have the exact change within the chasms of their purses.

Bad News for Bob

Some of the funniest times of my life have happened at church.

Maybe it's because it's usually so serious, that anything remotely embarrassing seems hilarious.

Maybe it's because church symbolizes the basis of our existence and there's a symbolism between humor and spirituality.

Maybe it's because it's just funny.

Take for example Bob Mahoney.

Bob and his family faithfully attended our church's appointed gatherings, including the evening services. On this particular night, Bob fell asleep during the sermon. He awoke to what he *thought* was the end of the sermon when everyone stands up and sings the invitational hymn. Not wanting to appear caught off guard, Bob grabbed a songbook and stood up. Just one problem. The invitation had not been extended. Bob was standing up all by himself.

What was Bob to do? In a split-second decision, he turned around, faced those behind him, stuck out his finger and began to count, like he was in charge of attendance for the back half of the auditorium. He didn't fool anyone, but it made it a lot more entertaining.

Then there was *the night* that our song leader, Bob
Johnson, fell asleep during the Sunday evening service.
Bob had been our song leader for some 13 decades,
and had the remarkable ability to sit on the front pew,
prop his head with his arm, which was resting on the
top of the pew, and go to sleep. From the back, it
looked like he was paying rapt attention. Only those
who preached or sat on the front row knew Bob's secret.
This narrowed it down considerably. Bob seemed to
always be able to wake up when the invitation was
extended, in time to grab his song book and lead the
chosen hymn of encouragement.

On this particular night, a distinguished professor was
presenting a slide show of his recent trip to the Holy
Land. There were a few problems here for Bob.

One, this was not the first, second, third or tenth time
that Bob had been in the audience for Professor
Dowdle's Holy Land post-trip slide show. Although the
slides were probably different, the Holy Land looked
the same.

Two, the lights were off.

Three, Professor Dowdle spoke in a monotone voice.
He spoke fast and ended abruptly.

This was all bad news for Bob.

So, Professor Dowdle's commentary on the slides went
something like this:

And in this slide, you see the Dome of the Rock, and in this slide you see a Nelson Glick pottery fragment, and in this slide you see our bus driver on a camel and if there's anyone subject to the invitation, please come as we stand and sing.

The lights came on, the congregation stood. Everyone except for Bob. He was still sitting in the front pew with his head propped up by his hand.

There was a long, awkward pause. No one sat close enough to the front to be able to poke Bob. Several decided to cough loudly. But Bob was far away in song leader la-la land.

My father, who is deaf in one ear and can't carry even a George Jones tune with the other, began clearing his throat. I panicked at the thought that **he** would start the song. Fortunately, two other folks started the song at that moment. *Unfortunately*, these two people were across the aisle from each other and started in different keys and tempos.

So, now, one half of the congregation is singing *Just As I Am* nine notes higher and half as fast as the other side. Bob's eyes popped opened. It took him a moment to realize what was happening.

He grabbed his songbook and leaped to the pulpit on stage. He began leading the song at the correct pitch and tempo, which was different from the other two renditions in progress. Members were switching from one group to another. So did Bob.

Then everyone got tickled. (My editor said that readers from the North and West wouldn't understand the idiom, *tickled*. This means they laughed out loud when they were supposed to be singing. It does not mean everyone was physically touched in such a way that they laughed. I think you could have figured this out on your own.) This was facilitated by Bob's hair sticking up on one side, the red hand print on the other side of his face and the look of horror in his eyes.

After the second verse, Bob ended the invitational hymn, walked down the steps and out the side door. We heard his car start up during the benediction. I guess he said his on the way home.

TIP: It's Not Wise to Insult Your Surgeon When You're In Surgery

I just participated in a video. It was a surprise video for a friend of mine, who I'll call Bob, on the occasion of his 40th birthday. I stood in front of his boyhood home and spun a few memories.

I was asked to participate because I'm Bob's longest friend. I don't mean long as in tall. I mean long as in he's known me longer than any other friend. I've known Bob since he was 0. I met Bob when he was one day old. I was still in the hospital myself at four days old.

From there, we attended the same nursery school, kindergarten, elementary school, Boy Scouts, Sunday School, basketball team and even sang in the same high school chorus that went to Europe.

Then our paths took separate directions. Bob became a doctor and I became his patient. We shared something I'll never forget. A surgery. *Mine.*

I broke my foot in my active role as a writer. Really. A truck was delivering some books to my office. I hopped up in the truck to look and, basically, sort of fell out of the back of the truck and broke a bone in my foot.

I called Bob. He looked at my foot, looked at my Minor Emergency Clinic X-Rays, smiled and said he needed to operate. This was not what I wanted to hear.

When the nurse gave me a form to fill out, I was a little perturbed. I mean it wasn't like Bob had just met me. I was his Boy Scout patrol leader, for Pete's sake.

I guess they detected my attitude when I filled in the birthday blank with, "Four days older than Dr. Bob."

When a nurse asked me about this, I informed her that Bob and I had known each other since our *first* hospital stay. Soon, several nurses were standing around, and I was telling them amusing childhood and adolescent stories about Bob. They were an enthusiastic audience.

I was beginning to feel a little recognition. I sensed special attention. I had some great, little known, seldom heard stories about Bob. They couldn't get enough of them. I enjoyed my new found prominence.

I didn't see Bob until I arrived in the Operating Room. Through his mask he said, "I understand you've been telling stories about me."

"Yeah," I chuckled, pleased with my recall and performance "How'd you know?"

"Oh, you've no idea how fast *real* doctor jokes travel through our hospital."

"Oh . . . Gee, Bob, sorry about that."

"Well, that's okay, Steve, old buddy. I mean it's only where I have to work and these are only the people who I'll see every day for the rest of my life."

"They weren't that bad. I just mentioned things like that time in the fourth grade when Harry Hutchison called us a name and we tried to look it up in your father's medical dictionary."

The anesthesiologist giggled under his mask.

The nurse wanted to know what the name was.

I was on a roll, even in the Operating Room. "Or the time you got the ball and started dribbling toward the wrong -"

"Let me just ask one question," Bob interrupted. "Do you remember many more of these high school stories?"

I laughed, "Oh yeah."

"Well, despite the havoc you've created for me, no one else knows them. So, if you even *think* about sharing any other embarrassing tales from my past, you can kiss your foot good-bye!"

If it's true that even a fool is considered wise if he remains silent, I chose not to be foolish, or walk with a limp.

How I Survived

A Defective Flat Top,
Corrective Shoes and
The Sparrow Reading Group

When I was in the fourth grade, I was the shortest
person in class, the youngest person in class and the
fattest person in class. I also wore corrective shoes. At
the time, there was only one style of corrective shoes -
big and ugly. Trudging down the green, white and
black tiled hallway with these clodhoppers on, it
sounded like a Clydesdale was loose in the building.
They weighted me down so that I was always the last
pick for relay races, baseball and about everything
else. Except *kickball*. I was a big hit in kickball.

The hairstyle of choice was a flat top. If you don't know
what that is, you could probably look it up in an
encyclopedia or look at Arsenio Hall. My problem was
that I had a cowlick (which has since gone to that great
barbershop in the sky). So my flat top did fine except
where my cowlick was in the front - there it looked
similar to the Great Pyramids. If you're keeping a list,
that's about five educational obstacles. Shortest, fattest,
youngest, corrective shoes and a defective flat top. I
was also dumbest. I know because my teacher told me

It's a little harder for a child today to guess where he stands academically. Our daughter brings home papers with stamps, animal stickers and smiley faces. It wasn't quite that subtle at Colonial Elementary in Memphis, Tennessee. We got an A, B, C, D or F - written in red ink. My friend, Grady Jim Robinson, said his teacher in Greenwood, Arkansas, was even more blunt. She told Grady's mom, "Mrs. Robinson, I'm sorry, but your son is *dumb*. We *might* be able to get him into the army. I don't know."

My friend, Mike Snider, said his Gleason, Tennessee, English teacher indicated he might be behind when he tried to give a high school book report on the same book for several years in a row. "What made it worse," Mike recalled, "was that it was *The Little Red Pony*."

Another time, Mike's Math teacher asked him, "Mike, how much is one-tenth of one percent?" Mike answered, "I don't know, ma'am, but it *couldn't* be much."

My fourth grade class had reading groups. There was the Cardinal reading group. Tad Fowler was in that group. Goes by John Fowler, M.D. now. That was the *A* group.

Then we had the Bluebird reading group. That was the *B* group. I remember that Becky Dacus was in that group. She lived across the street from me and talked me into eating mud one day, but I digress.

Then there was the Sparrow reading group. They
might as well have called it the *Stupid* Group. There
were only two of us in it. A fellow named Kenneth and
me. I'm not saying Kenneth was dumber than I was,
but he *was* older.

At the end of the school year, my parents came in my
room, sat down on either side of me on my army bunk
bed and reflected on my less than stellar academic
year. "Perhaps you just need to repeat the fourth grade
so you can be with children your own age," my mother
suggested. The *perhaps* was an indicator that that's
what they wanted me to do and they hoped I'd accept
that decision in a mature manner.

I stuck my head under my pillow and said, "Why don't
you just get a gun and put me out of my misery before
I'm humiliated in front of every kid in our
neighborhood."

They said something about "that's the attitude" and I
repeated the fourth grade.

The first day of fourth grade, second time around, my
new fourth grade teacher, Mrs. Riley, stood behind me
and watched me during art. She commented on the
lovely fish, which would have been great if I hadn't
been drawing a scuba diver at the time. But as she left,
she commented, "You can do it." I remember looking
up, "I can?"

No one had ever said that to me before except my
parents, and I figured *they* had to. That's something all
parents are required, by parental code, to say to their
kids.

I thought, "Hey, Mrs. Riley is smart. She's a teacher and
you don't just walk into those positions. If she says I can
do it, maybe I can. Unless, of course, she just doesn't
know me well enough yet." In which case I fully
expected her to come back to my desk in a few days
and say, "Steve, do you remember a few days ago I
told you that you could do it? Well, I was wrong. You
can't do it."

And then fate took a hand. Our class had officers:
President, Vice President, Secretary, Treasurer,
Sergeant at Arms, Lobbyists, Senators, Representatives,
Senate Minority Whip and Chaplain. The Chaplain led
the Pledge of Allegiance every day and a song like
"My Country Tis of Thee."

We also had an honor system in the form of paper
flowers in paper flower pots on the bulletin board.
Pulling a flower meant that you broke the conduct code
and were pretty sure that Mrs. Riley saw you. When
Mrs. Riley left the room and then returned, she would
often ask, *Does anyone need to go pull a flower?*

Several would reluctantly march over to their flower
pots and pull a flower. If you pulled five flowers in a
week, Mrs. Riley would send a note enclosed in black

construction paper home with you which said, "Bobby had to pull five flowers this week." Our parents would have to sign it and return it to Mrs. Riley, often with a note hinting that they had beat the child in question severely and it would not happen again without loss of at least one extremity.

Harry Hutchison was our class Chaplain and Harry had to pull five flowers in a week. Everyone knew that you were just not Chaplain material if you had to pull five flowers in a week, so Harry had to step down as Chaplain. I was nominated to run for Chaplain. Of course, almost everyone else already had some type of position. I won the election.

Actually, I edged by Kenneth in a run-off.

But Kenneth got the last laugh. He became an air traffic controller.

The Ultimate Threat –
Your Permanent Record

I remember once, right before graduation, our school superintendent, Dr. Bowie, was nervous about the fact that some of the class members might perform a Senior prank. There had been all types in the past. One year, the Seniors put a teacher's car on the roof. Another year, the Seniors had mounted a huge concrete, six foot high "70" in front of the school.

In an attempt to nip a senior prank in the bud, Dr. Bowie called a Senior Class meeting. We knew what was coming and we respected Dr. Bowie for his skill of persuasion. He was good. But we were Seniors.

I remember being in his office once. I forget the infraction, but someone had violated a school policy. Dr. Bowie assembled an office full of boys and threw us an administrative knuckle ball. Even though he was in an adversarial position, watching him at work was sheer entertainment.

"Okay, boys," he began. "I think you know why you've been called in here. Because one of you sitting in this office broke a sacred school rule. Now I'm pretty sure I know who it is. As a matter of fact, I have it on good authority who actually did it. But before I single out that person, I'm going to give him the opportunity to admit that he made a mistake. I'm not saying that he won't be punished, but I *am* saying that I'll take it into consideration that *he* told *me*, instead of me having to embarrass him. It takes a *man* to admit that he made a mistake and own up to it.

"But that's what I'm asking you to do, and believe me, that's the *best* thing you can do. That's the *only* thing you can do. Because if I have to confront you with it, then there's nothing I can do to help you. You've tied my hands. I don't want that, and you don't want that.

"So, I'll tell you what we're going to do. We're going to start here with Harry, and go all the way around the room. I want you to tell me whether you did or you didn't do it. If we get all the way around the room and this person has not admitted it - well, we'll just have to go to Plan B, but I hope and pray it doesn't get to that point. So Harry, let's start with you."

Harry: "I didn't do it, sir."

"Dr. Bowie?"

"Yes, Bob?"

"I did it."

Like I said, Dr. Bowie was good.

I used this technique years later in my capacity as the director of a one week junior high church camp at Camp Wyldewood in Arkansas. "Okay, boys, someone flushed an orange down the commode and it's all stopped up and running over. Now I think I know who it is, but before I pinpoint the guilty flusher, I'm going to give him an opportunity to come clean."

To my amazement, it worked! Larry confessed, just like a Perry Mason movie. He said he thought it would make things smell better. I'm not sure what I would have done if Larry hadn't stepped forward.

"Okay boys, I'm going to give that guilty flusher yet a *thirteenth* chance to confess."

In this case, getting the orange flusher to step forward wasn't as satisfying as I'd hoped. Perry Mason never had to de-orange a toilet.

Meanwhile, our Senior Class is awaiting Dr. Bowie to tell us not to pull any pranks. We knew what was coming and he knew we were waiting for his best pitch, with several years of batting practice.

"Class," he began, with the seriousness of Al Gore at, well, at anything, "I'm very concerned about something, and I wanted to tell you exactly how I feel. It's come to my attention that a *few* of you, not the majority of you by any means, but a few of you are considering playing a Senior Prank."

Snicker, giggle, whisper.

"Well, I hope this is just a rumor. We've had Senior Pranks in the past and they've always gotten out of hand. So, I want to tell you as directly as I know how, *don't attempt a Senior Prank.* "

Frankly, I was disappointed. That was the best he could do? This was embarrassing. But actually, what could he do? I mean we were graduating, and once we had graduated, that was -

"Now perhaps you've heard that once you graduate, the school has no power . . . no recourse . . . no authority. Maybe you heard that there's nothing the school can do to you once you receive your diploma."

That's exactly what we knew. He couldn't touch us. He might as well admit it and maybe we'd go easy on him graduation night.

"So, maybe you don't fully understand your PERMANENT RECORD."

What?

"Your permanent record goes to your employer when requested. It goes to your college. It even goes to the military. It can be requested for your summer jobs during college. It's a part of what all these groups use in making decisions about you. This permanent record follows you around - for the rest of your life.

"Yes, your grades have been posted, but your permanent record is ongoing. And rest assured, we'll list every detail of any Senior Prank and put it in your Permanent Record where it will stay forever.

"So, let me ask you, is one night's pleasure worth that kind of risk? I would hate to think that what you did following graduation could put a black mark on your Permanent Record for your entire career."

We believed him. What can I say? The man was good. I'm past my 20th year reunion, and I still think about my Permanent Record.

Somewhere there are brain cells in the cavity of my cranium that are thinking that one day I'll be offered a Big Kahuna type job. Like the one where I'll get a Lexus 400, fly First Class, sit in the box seats, actually have the need for a financial advisor and can buy toothpaste without looking at the price.

Then on my tenth day, the boss will come in, explain that he just received my Permanent Record and the deal's off.

Unnatural Gas

As I was leaving my office not long ago, I smelled something at the foot of the stairs. It was a smell that shouldn't have been there. It smelled like gas. I investigated for a few minutes.

I went out of the building and came back in and smelled. I went up the stairs, came back down and smelled. There was definitely an odor there. I just couldn't decide exactly what it was or where it was coming from.

On my way home, I contemplated the situation and decided that I should call Bob, my old college roommate and friend of over two decades. He also owns the building.

"Hello."

"Hi, Bob. I just wanted to tell you that as I was leaving your building tonight, I smelled something."

"What was it?"

"Well, it smelled like gas to me, but I don't want to be an alarmist. It was probably nothing. But I feel better knowing that you know about it."

"Let me get this straight. You called to tell me that you may have smelled gas in the building, but not to worry about it."

"That's right."

At this point, Bob recalls, "While Williford cuddled up to his pillows on the couch and watched TV, I called my General Manager and said, 'Keith, Steve thinks he smelled gas in the building. You live closer than I do. Would you go over there, check it out and give me a call?'

"A few minutes later, I get a call from Keith, 'Bob, it's really strong. I've already called Memphis Light, Gas and Water.'

"Okay, well, be careful. Don't turn the lights on and open the windows.

"At that point, I raced the 12 miles to my office and found a Memphis Light, Gas and Water truck in front with its lights flashing. Keith had opened all the windows and doors in the building.

"For the *first* hour, we checked the downstairs and didn't find anything. We didn't find anything from a gas point of view, that is. What the service representative *did* find were a couple of code violations which caused him to shut off heaters until repairs were performed. For the *next hour*, we went upstairs and crawled down the hall on our hands and knees in the dark, smelling under doors for gas. Then I got the master key and we opened office doors and checked each furnace individually. As we opened each furnace door, we didn't find gas, but again the service person found violations which were going to cost quite a bit of money.

"As we went down to the foot of the stairs, it hit me, '*I know what this is!* This isn't gas.' I looked at the MLG&W service representative and Keith. 'Do either of you know what this is?' They shook their heads and waited for my response. 'Well, I'll tell you what this is. This is cat urine.' (Author's note: Actually, I don't know that he said *urine*, but I'll go with it.) I encouraged the utility service representative and Keith to join me on my hands and knees and stick their noses to the carpet like I had done, but they were reluctant to do so."

About three hours after I initially called Bob, I received a phone call from him.

"Hi, Steve. What are you doing?"

"Oh, just watching a little of the ball game and eating popcorn."

"Oh, that's nice. Sounds like a relaxing evening."

"Yeah. Pretty relaxing."

"Do you want to know what I've been doing?"

"Sure."

"I've been crawling around in the dark on my hands and knees watching an MLGW service representative write me up for faulty equipment and discovering that after three hours, it wasn't natural gas at all. It was cat urine."

"Uh-oh."

"It turns out that a cat decided to mark his territory, the territory being our building, and some of his *marking* went under the door and landed on the stairway."

"Uh-oh. Well, look on the bright side. Aren't you glad there wasn't a gas leak!"

"Cat urine, Steve. I've been crawling on my hands and knees for three hours smelling cat urine."

"Uh-oh."

"Yeah," Bob continued, "the service person began to write some notes on a form and I asked, 'How are you going to file the report? Are you going to actually use the words *cat urine?*'

"The service person chuckled and said, 'No, I wouldn't do that. I'll have to think of something else. Meanwhile, I'm just making the notations of all the repairs that you'll need to make in the next five days. ' "

"Uh-oh."

Tips on Social Graces

As I find myself in public places like restaurants, stadiums, office buildings, auditoriums, airplanes and PTA meetings, it has become apparent that a few of us need a refresher course on public *do's* and *don't's*. It is very important that you read this. If you received this book as a present, you may soon understand why. Or, you may need to share these tips with a friend to keep him or her alive.

Tip: Never allow other human beings see you floss. If they do, give them $100 and apologize. Flossing, like other bodily responsibilities, is necessary, but can't be appreciated by anyone else.

Tip: Do not groan, sing, talk or whistle while you floss. If someone sees you do this, give me $100. Give them something substantial, like your refrigerator or stairmaster.

Tip: Never put your finger inside your nose in public. If it itches really bad, say "Look, isn't that John Grisham?" and take a quick scratch.

Tip: Blowing into a Kleenex so long that people speculate if part of your brain may have sprayed out is too long.

Tip: If you yawn without covering your mouth, you are doing those around you a terrible disservice. If you make a noise when you yawn in public, you are an evil person.

Tip: If you chew gum with your mouth open, especially at the theater, church or office, people will eventually do you harm.

Tip: If you cough without covering your mouth, be advised that you resemble a barking dog.

Tip: If your date or someone you might see while with your date should wear something you find particularly appealing, an appropriate response is not *Whoa, Doctah!*

Tip: Commenting on a stranger's food in a restaurant is in bad taste. No matter how badly you want to tell Myra to look at someone's chicken salad you're passing on the way to your table, don't.

Tip: Walking for exercise in a mall is acceptable. Power walking in a mall during shopping hours is resented by everyone else in the mall. One day they will rise up against you as you pass an exit.

After the Kiss

Bob Brown shared the story of his father's embarrassing mishap in church. When finished helping with communion, his father sat down beside Bob's mother and did what he always did when he sat down beside her - gave her a hug and a little peck on the cheek. Then he looked up and saw his wife on the row in front of him . . .

Is it Nervous in Here or am I Just Hot?

Mike Frihart recounted his first time to step behind the pulpit as a volunteer replacement for the preacher. "I don't remember saying this, but I was told by *several* members of the audience, that shortly after I began speaking, I asked that pertinent question, 'Is it nervous in here, or am I just hot?'"

Mike told of another time when the preacher was replaced by a young man who was also nervous. So nervous, as a matter of fact, that the color drained from his face "in about the first 30 seconds." He began to sweat profusely. "After about two minutes, he announced, 'I'm going to leave now. And I'm not coming back.'"

Members of many congregations all over the world have no doubt prayed for those very words to be uttered from their pulpit.

Parable of The Coke Machine

In Sunday School, we were studying a time when Jesus talked to a rich man. In an attempt to present a current example, our Sunday School teacher told of visiting an old high school friend who had become wealthy. The evidence he gave for that was that his friend had an actual Coke machine in his house.

Being the serious students my fellow classmates are, one asked if the teacher's friend needed another friend. Another pointed out that there were obviously many rich people in Memphis, as evidenced by all of the Coke machines on front porches.

Then a debate ensued as to whether the Sunday School teacher's friend actually owned the machine or leased it and which was more prestigious. One group of scholars thought owning it showed more financial savvy, while another significant contingency thought that leasing it showed that Coca-Cola took his account more seriously.

People have various views of wealth. Andy Rooney once described being rich as throwing soap away after the letters wore off.

My mother recently referred to a family as living an opulent lifestyle because they put their towels in the clothes hamper after using them only once.

I've heard it said before that wealth is only a state of mind. Right. Tell that to the IRS. Tell that to Master Card. Tell that to your spouse.

I think by this time our Sunday School teacher was in doubt over his Coke machine illustration. Maybe, instead, he should have talked about his friend's really big freezer.

Bob's Belated Underwater Discovery

After Bob, the guest preacher, finished his sermon, he was asked to baptize a woman, which he did. Since the stairs were slippery, he held the woman's arm and walked the steps with her to her dressing room.

However, he couldn't stay over there. He had to go to his dressing room on the other side of the baptistry, quickly get dressed, go downstairs and shake hands with congregation members as they left.

Normally, all he would have to do is re-enter the baptistry and walk to the other side, behind the closed curtains. But this baptistry didn't have curtains. Just some artificial plants at the front of the baptistry.

Bob knew he was stuck. So, he did what seemed to be the most logical thing to do. During the announcements, he slithered back down the stairs, and swam *underwater* to the other side. As he was swimming underwater to the other side, he happened to look at the wall of the baptistry facing the auditorium.

It was then that Bob made the discovery.

What Bob saw when he looked at the wall was hundreds of people looking back at him.

The wall was glass.

Bob's mouth dropped like a Big-Mouthed Bass and about drowned.

It's a good thing he didn't. Everyone was laughing too hard to help.

Dressed to Chill

I'm on my way to Chicago - one of the coldest cities in the nation today. As I watched the Weather Channel while dressing, I kept seeing "jet cold streams" over Chicago.

The temperature levels kept getting lower into minus digits the higher up the map - Chicago was coldest of those columns - at minus 10.

I put on another pair of socks.

The weather person began talking about wind chill - "And in Chicago, the wind chill makes it feel like **40 below!"**

I put on a heavy T-shirt.

As the weather person began describing conditions for St. Louis, he said, "That's cold alright. But look on the bright side, you could be in *Chicago!"*

I put on my heaviest sweater over my thickest winter shirt.

"We have some scenes of some winter activity," the weather prognosticator continued. "Wait till you see what they're having to put up with in Chicago." I sat on the bed and saw snow - in the air, on the ground, on people, under cars. "It's so bad, even the police are staying indoors!"

I looked into my closet for anything else I could put on. I found a sock hat. I reached for my long underwear, I got a second pair of gloves. I pulled out my overcoat and put the heavy lining in. I wrapped a scarf around my neck.

When I reached the airport waiting room for the Chicago flight, I surmised that everyone else had seen those same reports. Everyone looked like relatives of the Michelin Tire character. Many held their arms straight out, because they had too many clothes on to bend them. Several men were standing up, due to the fact that they couldn't sit down.

When we began to board, it took about eight days for everybody to remove their outerwear and stow it.

Referring to the extra pounds of clothes, passengers mumbled, "Really cold up there." As they sort of slid into their seats, they asked, "Did you see that weather report?"

The pilot just now came on, "Well, folks, we just received word that the weather has warmed up in Chicago." A plane full of overstuffed Southern passengers sat silently and acutely uncomfortable. "Yeah, it's a real heat wave . . . all the way up to minus five."

We felt validated. Hot, uncomfortable, stuffed between the arm rests of our seats, unable to move, our circulation cut off to our extremities, sweating in puddles, but validated.

Literary Lesson from the Collegedale Police

I called Arcata Graphics Book Group in Kingsport, Tennessee this morning to check on a book project. At least I thought I was calling Arcata.

The phone was answered by a low, serious voice:

"Collegedale Police Department."

"Uh, I think I've got the wrong number."

"What number were you trying to reach, sir?"

"Arcata Graphics Book Group."

"No sir, they don't arrest people and we don't read books."

Life's Untrues

There are certain embarrassing trues in the world. For example, if you chew gum when you go to bed, you'll wake up with it in your hair.

If you wear a new white shirt to a restaurant, you'll drop a big glob of spaghetti on it.

But just as there are certain trues in the world, there are also certain *untrues*. Consider the following:

"We're not lost. I don't need to stop and ask directions."

"The doctor will be with you shortly."

"The cleaners must have shrunk my pants."

"If you'll let me stay up 10 more minutes, I promise I'll go right to bed."

"Taste this. It's not hot."

"We don't need to make reservations - there'll be plenty of vacancies."

"They'll be gone before you know it."

"I'll be ready in five minutes."

"If you'd ever like to borrow it, don't hesitate to call."

"It looks like sunburn, but it will turn to tan."

"It was no trouble at all."

"We've got plenty of gas."

"I'm sorry, Mr. Jones is in a meeting."

"Honey, I wasn't looking at her. She just reminds me of your Aunt Jo."

"We just happened to be in the neighborhood."

"I'll lose some weight by the time I have to wear it."

"Come on in. The water's great."

"Of course, we love meat loaf."

"Maybe my coupon hasn't expired."

"I'm not jealous."

"One size fits all."

"Returns with sales slips gladly accepted."

"The new hair cut will look a lot better when it's washed."

"A baby sitter on New Year's Eve shouldn't be that hard to find."

"I love to go camping."

"Of course I'll be just as romantic after we're married."

"If you're ever in town, we'd love for you to stay with us."

"Your children were angels while you were gone."

"I'm not mad."

"There's plenty of ice to make ice cream."

"Oh, a vacuum cleaner. It's a wonderful present."

"I'll bring the book back as soon as I finish it."

"I'll pay you right back."

"You look great in horizontal yellow and black stripes."

A Dachshund Can Make You Go Blind

Dachshunds aren't real dogs. Real dogs sleep on the porch and go *woof*, not *yap-yap-yap-yap*. You can't hurt a real dog's feelings. Oh, okay, maybe for a minute, but the next minute, you've been forgiven. A Dachshund holds a grudge - for life.

We bought a Dachshund a few years ago. One morning, Pumpkin - the Dachshund who slept *in the bed with us* - caused me to have a severe panic attack. I woke up and couldn't see. Everything was dark. Then I felt something over my eyes. Pumpkin was sleeping on my *face!*

Dachshund owners also have to learn a new way to walk. *The Dachshund Shuffle.* Because Dachshunds are so low to the ground, their owners can never again take full strides. Instead, they have to take steps which are shorter and lower to the ground.

This is usually learned only after stepping on the little hotdog or accidentally drop kicking it over the coffee table.

When we moved to the country, I was concerned that the circling hawks were planning on making Pumpkin an evening meal, so I bought a bodyguard for

Pumpkin - a German Shepherd. I thought it would be nice protection for my family, too. My wife named our guard dog - Precious.

Pretty intimidating, huh? Not Fang or Death or Bullet - Precious. Can you see it, "Kill, Precious!" Pumpkin growled at Precious when she was a puppy and even when Precious was full grown, she feared Pumpkin's growl. All Pumpkin had to do was show Precious a little tooth and Precious folded like a house of cards.

I'm sorry to say that Pumpkin has gone on to become a heavenly hot dog. Andrea cried for weeks and still can't look at his picture. So, we then got another dog for Precious - another German Shepherd - Mike (*I* named him).

In retrospect, the name may have been a mistake. Our next door neighbor is also named Mike. It gets confusing. I'll whistle and yell, "Supper Mike!" I'll hear, "Thanks, Steve, but I've already eaten."

You might ask, "How did Mike become a part of your family?" I had accepted the invitation of a friend's father to come and speak to a church youth audience. After I declined the fee (it was *for a church!*), the friend's father, Neil, said, "Well you've got to take something - here take my dog!" I assured Neil that I sensed his gratitude and left town without his dog.

A few weeks later, I got a call from Northwest Airlines saying, "We have a package for you."

"Thank you, I'll pick it up in the morning."

"Uh, you'd better come now."

Neil's dog had puppies. Guess what Neil sent? A German Shepherd puppy, Mike. Mike grew to weigh over 100 pounds.

One day in the heat of our Mississippi summer, Mike and Precious were looking for a cool place to sprawl. After a careful search of the grounds, they determined that spot to be the Impatiens bed I planted. This bed was my pride and joy. It took me hours to plant a couple of hundred Impatiens all around our Sweet Gum tree. I was expecting a call from *Southern Living* any day.

Unfortunately, they soon became the variety, "Impatienus Flat as a Pancake." When I drove up and saw Precious and Mike cooling their canine heels in that flattened flower bed, I chased them around the house a few times until I ran out of threats. I finally had to sit down on the car to rest and they promptly dropped on the Impatiens to recuperate - until I broke the sound barrier: *"Mike, you good-for-nothing, flea-bitten, tick-infested, bone-headed excuse for an animal!"*

From next door, I heard, "I'm sorry, did I miss supper again?"

Somehow I still blame Pumpkin for those flowers. After all, if we hadn't bought him, we wouldn't have needed

Precious or her playmate Mike and the Impatiens would have never been squashed.

I'm sure Pumpkin heard my roar, saw the damage and heisted a leg in my honor.

Waiting for the Garage Door to Open

One day not too long ago my wife called and said, "You need to come home *right now!*"

I dropped the phone and rushed home.

When I got home, she said, "It's the garage door."

"The what?"

"The garage door."

"What about it?"

"It keeps going up and down."

I opened my mouth; she intercepted.

"I know, that's what garage doors do, but not by *themselves!*"

I looked at her closely. Had she seen one too many *Full House* episodes? I've heard that could do it to you.

"Just sit down in the kitchen and wait."

I sat at the kitchen table, waiting for the garage door to open by itself.

As I sat there, I had time to think. I thought of my friend, David LaVelle, the orthopedic surgeon, operating on somebody's broken tibula. And of my friend, Fred Smith, the founder of Federal Express, putting together a multi-billion dollar deal with Japan or China or both. I thought of fellow Mississippian, John Grisham, author of *The Firm* , *The Client* and other mega-whoppers, listening to Paramount ask him if it could buy the movie rights for a book he *hadn't even written yet* for $3.75 million. I thought of President Bill Clinton, my contemporary, busy creating global policy. I wondered if *they* ever sat at their kitchen tables and waited for their garage doors to open. Does the White House have a garage? I made a mental note to ask Bill.

So I waited. Long enough to think all of that.

To my surprise, I heard the garage door go up!

I ran to the door and watched it ascend. I looked outside and there was no one there. Only Mike and Precious, our two German Shepherds. When you have two German Shepherds, you don't expect to see anyone just hanging around.

This phenomenon repeated itself several times.

I looked at Andrea. She was smug.

I thought about possible garage door explanations with my vast array of technical ignorance.

I reflected on a day in college when my clock radio began to hum. As I mentioned this problem to my roommates, John Durham, a neighbor from down the hall, sauntered into our dorm room. He examined the radio, listened to it and with a sincere and confident voice announced, "I'll fix it."

John disappeared with my radio under his arm. About an hour later, he reappeared with a shoe box. He placed the shoe box on my desk. It was my radio - in a thousand pieces. John had taken my humming, but *working*, clock radio down to his room, turned on *Perry Mason*, and proceeded to unscrew and unplug anything he could find.

"I couldn't fix it," he announced, and walked out.

I understand that John now works for the phone company in Birmingham.

But I digress.

Perhaps it was a frequency from someone's cellular phone that caused the garage door to go up. Did that mean that every time someone called Harry's Plumbing Service mobile phone, our garage door would go into action?

Or maybe it was from some kid's Nintendo game. When he put in something like *Journey to Arkon* and hit the photon torpedo switch, the garage door switched on.

About that time, Mike walked past the garage with something in his mouth. I didn't have anything else to do, so I engaged in a conversation with Mike.

"Hey, buddy. How's man's best friend? Are you keeping an eye on this garage door? Say, what's that you've got in your mouth? It looks like - Aaaaiiiiiiiiiihhhhhhhh!"

As I've reconstructed the crime scene, Mike apparently walked into the open garage and moseyed past the car. He noticed the window was down and stuck his head in to look around. Big German Shepherds can do that. They can do whatever they want to do.

Mike saw the opener, thought it looked interesting, if not tasty, and snatched it. As he occasionally munched on it during the afternoon, the garage door went up and down, for his added entertainment, like a crazed dixie cup-bobbing bird.

So much for the Nintendo theory.

So much for the garage door opener.

Your Legal Rights

On those rare occasions that I face the darker side of man and lose money, the first question that I hear is not:

(a) "That must have been a terrible experience. Are you okay?"

(b) "This won't diminish your positive outlook on life will it?"

(c) "Do you need to borrow some money?"

Instead, the question I most frequently hear is:

"Did you have a *contract*?"

"No," I always answer. This is when the questioner shakes his/her head and clicks his/her tongue.

Well, I've been cheated for the last time. I'm going to become pro-contract. I'm going to get *everything* in writing.

- I'm going to come to terms with my barber before said haircut and sign a letter of agreement.

- I'm going to draw up a contract with my cleaners not to shrink my pants.

- Before our child attends Vacation Bible School, I will draft a contract for Bible stories to be covered.

- I'll be sending Leno and Letterman contracts regarding our entertainer-audience agreement.

- When the dentist says, "No cavities," I'll smile and say, "Sign here."

Highly Honed Trading Skills

You can embarrass yourself anywhere. Even at a football game. You can actually embarrass yourself just buying a ticket to the game.

My friend, Ray, and his wife Ruby were going to see a college football game.

"But we don't have tickets!" Ruby pointed out.

"No problem," Ray replied.

"Won't that be inconvenient about the time we want to enter the stadium?"

"We'll simply procure them at the stadium."

"Isn't that a bit risky, not to mention expensive? We'll have to pay scalper's prices to get any tickets."

This got Ray's attention, because if Ray's nothing else, he's **cheap.**

"Obviously, dear, you are not aware of my keen, highly honed, negotiating skills."

"You mean *finely* honed?"

"Whatever."

So Ray and Ruby park in the front yard-turned parking lot of Jareeb, who parks cars with space the width of a ritz cracker between them. They make their pilgrimage to the stadium which is no more than 20 football fields away.

"What now, oh highly honed one?"

"Well, we'll just mosey around and check out the action," Ray said as he hitched up his pants and buttoned his wallet pocket.

It seems that the few tickets which were available were going at a premium slightly less than Ray paid for the family vacation. Game time was approaching. Ruby looked grim. Jareeb was back at the lot squeezing yet one more car into the space of a shopping cart.

"I could feel the pressure," Ray recounted. "I saw this guy holding up two tickets. This was no ordinary man. This was a mountain of a man, a building of a person, a -"

"Okay, we get the *Big John* idea. Hurry up and get on with the story," Ruby urged.

"Uh, right . . . so -"

"I'll take it from here," Ruby smiled. "So Ray nudges me and says, '*Show time,*' and walks over to this huge, scary wrestler-looking guy.

" 'How much you want for your tickets?' Ray asks him.

" ' Eighteen dollars,' the guy says.

"Ray says, 'Okay, I'll tell you what I'm going to do. The game's about to start, so I'll give you $30 for both of them. Take it or leave it.'

The man nods and holds out his big hand.

"So Ray gives the man $30 and he gives Ray the two tickets and then it *hits* Ray! The guy was going to sell him *both tickets* for $18! He says, 'I just paid you $12 more than you were asking, didn't I?'

"The guy breaks into a huge crocodile smile and nodded. 'Yeah, I thought I was going to have to eat these tickets. I'd have probably *given* them to you.' "

That's part of the reason Ray now has season tickets, to avoid such scenarios and reminders. But as long as Ruby continues to call him *highly honed one*, I don't think it's working.

How to Pass the Time in the Waiting Room

I'm here in a doctor's office waiting room. What are you supposed to do to pass the hours in a waiting room? In order to avoid going crazy and having to pay an additional psychiatric bill, I decided to create *The Top 10 Activities for Patients in a Doctor's Waiting Room*:

#10: Find rude cartoons about nurses and doctors and tape them under the counter.

#9: Look around. This gets old after an hour. But you can do this again after you get through sleeping and see who's new, who's gone and who's sleeping. You can also check to see who's expired (which is a medical term for croaked). If you happen to find an overly stiff patient, this is a bad sign. It will certainly mean a longer wait.

#8: Do leg exercises. This has a couple of drawbacks. It tends to trip other patients walking close by and causes you to get sweaty (you can do a lot of leg lifts in two hours) which may result in a faulty diagnosis or a heart attack before you ever get to see the doctor. Or worse, you might have to come back.

#7: Talk on a cellular phone. However, while it's impressive, it's also expensive and annoying.

#6: *Pretend* to talk on your cellular phone. This is just as annoying but less expensive. It can also be embarrassing if the phone happens to ring while you're talking away.

#5: Hoard all the magazines. There's not much point in this activity, but after awhile, waiting rooms can leave you hardened.

#4: Slip a whoopee cushion under a fellow patient's chair when he or she has to get up to answer some insurance question.

#3: Sit close to the check-in window and begin a coughing, wheezing, sneezing and groaning frenzy. It should get you bumped up on the waiting list. You should be able to wear them down after an hour or so. It might also clear out the waiting room.

#2: Bring a stop watch and whistle. Tape a poster board on the wall next to you marked, *Current Waiting Time.* Update it every 15 minutes. Blow the whistle and announce the update.

#1: Be a leader. Distribute bingo cards. Have some group fun. Winners can choose from these fabulous prizes: a 1982 *Consumer Guide Magazine,* half of a pamphlet on *Regularity and You,* the code for the gate to the doctor's parking lot, your doctor's beeper number or all the prescription samples you can stuff into a rubber glove.

How to Explain Things To Your Child

The fact that Brittney was going to Kindergarten at the same location that I had attended a few decades earlier gave me a sense of connectivity that transcended our age difference. It was a bond, something that we would always share. I wanted to make sure she understood.

"Brittney, do you realize that I went to Kindergarten here, too?"

"Yes."

"And I played on the same playground, and learned some of the same things that you'll learn."

"Yeah."

"Well, isn't it great that we both went to the same Kindergarten!"

"Yeah. Daddy?"

"Huh?"

"Was Miss Paige your teacher too?"

"Uh, no."

"Yeah, she was probably teaching the Pre-School class then."

"Well, actually, Paige wasn't teaching yet when I was here."

Actually, Miss Paige was not even **born** yet, and would not be born until about the time I entered Junior High, but I didn't want to lose that feeling of connectivity. I wasn't dishonest with my answer. She *wasn't* teaching when I was there. If you're not born, you can't teach.

Okay, so I hedged. I avoided. But I'll tell you one thing I didn't do. I didn't bond. Brittney's interest was not whether I went to her Kindergarten or had served two terms in the Oval Office. She was interested in weightier issues.

"Can I have my snack now?"

"No, your snack's for Snack Time."

"Do you have a piece of gum?"

"Yes."

"Can I have it?"

"Yes."

"Can we listen to my *Wee Sing* tape now?"

"Sure."

"Thanks Daddy. Going to Kindergarten is fun isn't it?"

"Yeah."

"Did your Daddy take you to Kindergarten on his way to work?"

"Yes he did."

"Then you know what I mean."

That conversation prompted me to want to make our commutes to school as meaningful as possible. I wanted it to be more than listening to the radio. I wanted it to be more than fun. I wanted it to be *educational*.

The next day, I seized the opportunity and enthusiastically pointed, "Do you know what we call those trees that are green throughout the year?"

There was only one thing wrong with my educational agenda. The student was less than thrilled. She was used to educating *me*. Still, she understood that the best tactic was to meet it head on and get it over with as quickly as possible.

"What?" she sighed.

"Those are evergreen trees," I exuded, " because they stay green all year long."

Brittney was quiet for awhile. "Well . . . really that's an old fashioned term like 'Thank you ever so much' or 'We're ever so grateful.' We don't use that word very much anymore. Next time, just say Pine Tree."

Maintaining the Family Safety Standard

I've always **prided** myself on being a cautious parent.

My wife **accuses** me of being a cautious parent.

As I see it, I've simply attempted to ensure the safety and well-being of our offspring while in our legal responsibility.

For example, I've always viewed putting rocks, nails, bugs, jewelry, small animals and keys in one's mouth as off limits for anyone under 45. Other hazards which require rules, in my opinion, include sharp objects, stairs, electrical outlets, seat belts, stun guns, Barry Manilow tapes, pools and sharp corners on furniture. As a result, *I* think I've saved us countless emergency room trips. Andrea thinks I've become a deeply rooted stick in the mud.

Ironically, during such time of child accident prevention, *my* accident rate has increased dramatically. Take the hummingbird feeder incident. I was on the ladder trying to hang the glass feeder and the next thing I knew *I* was in the emergency room.

Then there was the falling off the back of a truck incident. I received a shipment of my books. I hopped in the back of the trailer to help unload them and -

okay, so I fell out of the back of the truck. Cost me a broken bone, an operation and a lot of head wagging by Andrea. I think I actually heard her giggle outside my hospital room.

There was also the time I tried pulling on the rope of the stuck garage door. It broke, I fell on my head, but I didn't tell anybody about it - until now. Maybe that's why I suffer recurring bouts of writer's block.

Now, here we are in Florida on one of our famous vacations. So far, through my careful safety precautions, Brittney has not slipped at the pool, bumped her head on the counter, fallen over the balcony, eaten any shells, stepped on a jelly fish or been swept off by a riptide.

I, on the other hand, have been sunburned, tripped over the hide-a-bed on the way to the bathroom and, most recently, bumped into an open cabinet door in our condo's kitchen, causing an 'L' shaped slice on my forehead. I had to use the family first aid kit I insisted we buy - on me. Upon seeing the latest bandage, Andrea shook her head and gave me the look, "I'm not going to say anything out loud, but I'm thinking it as hard as I can."

It's not easy setting the safety standard for the rest of the family while steadily injuring my body parts from head to toe. It's embarrassing. It also tends to diminish my credibility.

Honey They Shrunk My Clothes

I've got to get a new cleaners. The one I use now keeps shrinking my pants. It's embarrassing.

While we were in Florida, Andrea looked over at me and made some comment that I would make a wonderful and *ample* meal for a family of sharks.

I tried to tell her that I wasn't fat. She didn't say a word. She just pointed to the top of my stomach - it was sunburned.

It's just very difficult for me to let go of some habits that have become too close to my heart. What is milk without doughnuts? What's cereal without a pop- tart? What's a banana without a split?

It's hard to go to the all-you-can-eat buffet and reach over the prime rib for some lime jello.

I should have understood when I saw subtle hints - the industrial strength sized cans of Slim Fast in the fridge. Or the framed photograph of Tommy Lasorda holding out his pants. Or Christmas gifts of holiday cottage cheese. Or the talking scales that say, "Get off! Get off!"

I guess I should have figured it out when my dockers no longer pleated.

I should have seen a clue when children looked at my shirt and told me that I was growing lint in my belly button.

This time I'm prepared for Florida. I'm eating salad and jello. I walk. I stairmaster. I have Slim Fast in the fridge. And most important, I'm going to put sunscreen on the top of my stomach.

Fill In the Blank Conversation

I have been told by many people who live in the Eastern, Western and Northern United States that those of us who live in the South speak with speed roughly equivalent to that of wood petrifaction.

I have been told even by my fellow Southerners that the pauses I insert between the beginning and end of my sentences are sufficient to go watch a short PBS documentary and not miss anything.

Contrast that with Tricia, a friend with roots and speech patterns from the Midwest. Tricia's speech pattern parallels the speed of the Road Runner, not stopping for little things like periods, paragraphs or subject changes. She is in warp drive to my stroll in the mine field pace.

Her speed makes my ears hurt. My pace makes her crazy. So she tries to help by finishing my sentences.

For example:

Steve: "It's such a pretty day, I was thinking about going . . ."

Tricia: "For a walk?"

Steve: "No."

Tricia: "On a trip?"

Steve: "No."

Tricia: "Home early?"

Steve: "No."

Tricia: "I give up, where?"

Steve: "I forgot."

A typical conversation goes like this:

1 second _._._._._._._._._._._._._._._._._._._. **10 seconds**

Tricia: I'm going to the condo in 2 weeks, I've been up since 4:30, I've washed 5 loads of clothes, took the kids to school and paid the bills. Are we still getting together this week-end? I've got to get some exercise today. How's your book coming?

Steve: Well, ...its..

Tricia: Not as easy as you thought?

Steve: Well, ...its..

Tricia: Going great and your almost through?

Steve: No, ...I was going to say that .... ..I've decided ....to .....

Tricia: Not finish it?

Steve: No.

1 second _._._._._._._._._._._._._._._._._._ **10 seconds**

Tricia: To work on something else?

Steve: No.

Tricia: Well, whatever you decide will be just fine, I'm sure. In the meantime, I'm going to go play tennis, then go to the ballet. I need to finish a book before I go. Then we leave for vacation tomorrow. We're going to Canada, then Alaska, then

Seattle, and on to a dude ranch. Where are you going on vacation?

Steve: Well, we were thinking of going . . .

Tricia: To Destin.

Steve: No.

Tricia: The Smokeys, right?

Steve: No, ... !"

Tricia: "Hawaii?

Steve: *No!!!!"*

Tricia: What? I'm just trying to carry on a conversation, but obviously you don't want to, so just forget it, but before I go, let me tell you about . . .

The Great Tomato Hope

Every year about Easter, I begin to feel the urge to get out the old hoe, buy some peat moss and carefully select some tomato plants. I faithfully water these tomato plants, watch them grow and am subsequently always disappointed by the meager, puny, embarrassing results.

Yet, like Charlie Brown who faithfully awaits the Great Pumpkin year after year, I hold the Great Tomato Hope.

I do all the right things. I watch *Victory Garden*. I built a raised garden bed. I read *Square Foot Gardening*. I bought a tomato cage. I got a drip-drop hose. I made a compost cage.

Of course, I have had my share of catastrophes - like last year when our two German Shepherds decided the coolest place in the yard was on top of the drip-drop hose under the tomatoes.

Then there was the year I sprayed the tomatoes with insecticide - I thought - okay, so it was Round-Up.

I got a tiller. I got manure. I got *The Tomato Book* at the Hardware Store. I looked at others' tomatoes until they started wanting to see mine.

This year, I'm pulling out all of the stops. I'm going to enroll in a gardening class.

I'm going to attend a Tomato Support Group.

"Hello, my name is Steve and I killed my tomatoes."

I'm installing a cyclone fence with razor wire around my garden.

I'm going to buy an electronic timer which waters the plants at precisely the moment they become thirsty.

At this rate, my tomatoes should be worth about $57 a pound.

If that doesn't work, I'll buy some tomatoes from the grocery and glue them on.

There's always next summer.

Why We Don't Own
A Lazy-Boy

I have a friend who I'll call Bob. Bob's wife, Mary, received a call last month from a college friend, explaining that she was going to get married in their city, and asking if she could stay with them the week-end prior to the blessed event.

Mary said that would be fine. She was looking forward to seeing her old friend after all these years.

A few days later, Mary's friend called back and asked if she could bring a couple of family members for the wedding. Mary said that would be great. Their house was not equipped with guest bedrooms, but they were welcome to sleep on the couch which made into a bed.

When the day of the visit arrived, Mary answered the door and greeted her friend. Her friend, an American Indian, sort of nervously giggled, "I think I brought the whole tribe." Only then did Mary see the cars and trucks which held 11 other family members, including the grandfather who could only say "Bye" in English.

Later in the day, the family went to Wal-Mart to get a few last minute wedding necessities, leaving Mary and the grandfather home alone. Communication quickly broke down.

"Would you like to watch TV?"

"Bye."

"Well, maybe TV is not such a good idea since you wouldn't understand the words."

"Bye."

"Is your chair comfortable?"

"Bye."

"If you get stuck in the Lazy-Boy again, just call me, okay?"

"Bye."

Then she remembered an Indian-related movie she had recorded. *Winds of War, Wings of an Eagle, Winds of a War Eagle* or something like that.

She turned the video on and went back to the kitchen. Some time after that, she heard the grandfather yell, and rushed back to the den. She found him *standing* on the Lazy-Boy. He was watching the scene of an Indian, fighting a bear with a spear, and was evidently shouting advice and encouragement to the Indian in the television.

Later, during supper, Mary's college friend said, "Grandfather told me that you showed him a movie about an Indian fighting a bear."

"Ask him how he liked it."

The grandfather's answer took about two minutes.

"He says it scared the crud out of him."

That evening, Bob and his family invited the group to attend an annual large religious gathering held in their city. About 10,000 were in attendance. The first thing that happened, as you might imagine, were some hymns. Then a sermon. Bob said that by this time, the grandfather was so deeply asleep, three out of four gerontologists would have put a tag on his toe.

The next order on the agenda was a gospel quartet. Bob said as soon as they began singing, the grandfather perked up. As the songs got livelier, so did grandpa. Next thing Bob knew, the grandfather had slipped past him into the aisle and was doing a really nifty and energetic Indian dance to the music. At least to the four or five thousand that could see him, he stole the show. He was headed down to the front to join the singers on stage when Bob caught up with him and walked him back to his seat.

Bob was not telling this in a disgusted, disgruntled, whiney, horrified, shell-shocked, thunderstruck, grudge holding, revenge seeking sort of way. He was telling it with a sense of awe. A respect for the grandfather's ability to engage and enjoy life as it came to him. An appreciation for the way the other relatives adapted to their living conditions and events.

My question is, how come *we* don't get any guests like that? I never look out and see four times more house guests than I expected. I never scare the crud out of my guests. None of our guests make a break for the stage.

But then again, we don't have a Lazy-Boy.

Embarrassing
but Entertaining

In these economically hard times, I feel called upon to help you, my fellow American consumer, save money. I see folks spending hard earned money for entertainment purposes. It may be a movie or a video or a ball game or a concert or the theater or even the circus.

This is totally unnecessary.

Especially when there is a form of free entertainment so close by. You can participate in any part of the country and it's absolutely free.

I take great delight in watching people get mad in public places. Not because of some deviant, pathological quirk, but for pure entertainment. I've been involved in Spot a Fit about 16 years, so let me give you rookies four prime places to begin this entertainment:

(1) **Golf courses**. Go to any golf course at any daylight hour and inside of 30 minutes, you will sight at least one good tantrum. The record number of tantrums sighted in an hour (TSH) was by Bill Rojensky in Phoenix, in 1987, on July 4, with temperature of about 160 or so. Bill's TSH record holds at 86.

Here are some things you might see at the golf course:

- A golfer who is wearing the finest clothes, best golf shoes and neatest bag, tees up his new ball, adjusts it half a dozen times, takes out his golf computer to tell him what club to use, settles into his stance which has been fine-tuned by several out-of-state golf clinics, rares back and . . . dribbles the ball seven feet off the tee. As the other golfers howl, he pounds his $400 dichromium cobalt driver into the ground like he was trying to ring the bell with a sledge hammer.

- I've seen golfers shank a ball, scream and then wrap a new five iron around a tree.

- I was playing with a guy once who was so miffed that he missed the green from 75 yards, he pulled out his irons, one by one, and slung them in all directions. Then he threw his putter in the same lake his ball went in. He had to chip and putt the rest of the holes with his sand wedge.

(2) **Traffic.** This one is almost too easy. You can spot a traffic tantrum in almost every outing. You could even cause someone to get angry, but this does not count as an official sighting. Easy targets are mothers running carpools. It doesn't take much to set them off. They're already on the edge.

If you're having trouble spotting a traffic tantrum, just follow anyone talking on a cellular phone.

They may not have one, but they're sure to cause one.

(3) **Standing in Line at the Department Store.**
They've been standing in line at Target for some 92 minutes. They are now within sight of the price scanner. Some may actually be making a move for their billfolds. Then the clerk picks up a "Mr. Car Deodorant" and passes it over the scanner and nothing happens. After she tries this for five minutes, she picks up the microphone, "Price check for Automotive."

An audible groan passes through the line. If the price check is closely followed by a customer who says (always in a nasal tone), "I thought that was on special," you know the microphone is about to be picked up again. Stay close to this line.

(4) **Waiting in the Fast Food Line.** The basic problem here is that you have two opposite sets of people coming in contact with each other.

You have one set that is in a hurry. That's why they're in the fast food take-out line.

The only problem is that they're being served by a set of people that is in absolutely no hurry at all. The fact that their customers **are** has no impact on their delivery of service.

They have also mastered that art of distorted public speaking, duplicated only by people inhaling helium and Northwest Airlines pilots at 30,000 feet. You're 100% assured of witnessing a real Big Mac Attack if, after waiting the average length of power of some third world countries, a customer is asked to "pull up and someone will be right out with your order."

Welcome to Disney Line

It's a question of the ages. Why does a family spend so much time

planning

anticipating

traveling to

and paying for a vacation

and then spend the entire time

arguing

holding grudges

and vowing to never, ever again go on a vacation?

A classic spot to Spot a Fit is Disney World. I know this one's expensive. As you may recall, I earlier mentioned the big advantage of Spot a Fit is that it's inexpensive. Big Deal. It's only money. Forget what I said before. You get what you pay for.

While you're in one of the many lines (They ought to rename it Disney Line. *If you put all our lines together, they'd wrap around the world! Come be a part of them!*), look at the faces of family members. At least

four out of every 11 will have unhappy faces. About
two out of every 17 will have that look of "Why did we
think this would be fun?"

Often these are parents of infants too young to even
know who Mickey Mouse is. I've always wondered
why parents would spend a couple of grand to show
their nine month old around Disney World. She or he
would be just as happy in the back yard or next door
playing in a sand box. That's probably what the kid is
thinking, "Next year, leave me next door in the sand
and *you* go stand in line!"

Eight out of nine parents have the frozen, but
determined expression that says, *We're going to have a
good time if it kills us.* If you look hard enough you'll
hear parents' little endearing vacation comments like,
"Wipe that look off your face before I do."

Occasionally, you'll be lucky enough to see something
more overt, like the wife screaming in the middle of
crowded Main Street, *Let's go home right now.
Nobody's having any fun and the lines are so long I
have to wait 30 minutes just to take Whitney to the
bathroom. Then she tells me she doesn't need to go.
Then after we've been in the Dumbo line for 50
minutes, she says she has to go!*

Meanwhile, back on Main Street, Whitney throws up on
her little brother.

This might be a good one for the video camera.

Blowing Smoke

When a lot of people think of Dr. Bob, they think of the many years he was a professor at my alma mater, David Lipscomb College in Nashville, Tennessee.

When I think of Dr. Bob, I think of flour.

The year was 1974. Walton Smith and Mark Jones (last names changed to prevent retaliation) were students in one of Dr. Bob's classes. Walton and Mark liked a good, practical joke.

That was later evidenced at their graduation by President Pullias' comments being pre-empted by "Looney Tunes" music ending with "that-that-that's all folks."

It was evidenced to me the time I needed a cigar. At the conclusion of our fraternity's pledge period, each current member would stand in front of his car, and solemnly shake hands, welcome and congratulate each pledge, while blowing cigar smoke in his face.

The pledges were almost to my car and I had accidently sat on my only cigar. I turned to Walton. "Walton, I need a cigar. Could you loan me one of yours?"

Walton grimaced, "Gee, Steve, I'd like to help you, but I only have one left, and I . . . "

"Please, Walton, I'd consider it a personal favor."

Walton pulled out a rich-looking cigar in a beautiful glass case. "Well, these are very special. Very rare. I was looking forward to . . . "

I eyed the cigar. The pledges were a car away. "I really *need* that cigar," I said in complete desperation. "Walton, they're almost here, *"PaLeeeese!"*

Walton shrugged, handed me the cigar. I thanked him profusely, lit the stogie and turned to greet the now-arrived pledges.

BOOM!

I didn't know what had happened at first. I'd never even thought of a cigar load - those little toothpick-like pieces of gun powder one can slip into a cigar, causing it to explode. At the present time, I was more concerned about whether my face had been blown off. It seems that Walton saw fit to insert an entire package of loads into my precious cigar, sufficient enough to burn the very hairs right out of my nose.

When the smoke cleared, the only thing left of the cigar was a little stub that extended in every direction.

But I digress.

As was told to me, Dr. Bob received a package one day during his lecture. It was a beautifully wrapped, courier delivered gift with a note that said, "Dear Dr. Bob, You had so much impact on me while I was at Lipscomb that I wanted to give you a little something back. Please take the time now to open your gift. It would mean that much more to me if your students could share in this moment. A happy alumnus."

Dr. Bob, normally a real stickler for maximizing class time, acquiesced for a grateful alum. He unwrapped the gift to discover a beautiful, cigar box. He turned the lever on top of the box and - well first let me explain what the box contained.

Rumor has it that Walton and Mark found an industrial strength metal spring - not unlike what you'd find in an old mattress. Next they cut a piece of plywood the exact dimensions of the cigar box and forced the spring down by pushing *hard* on the plywood. While one held the plywood and spring in this position, the other filled the box up with as much Martha White's Self-Rising Flour as was humanly possible. With one coordinated, quick motion, they closed the lid on the box and fastened the lever shut.

Back to Dr. Bob. After opening the lever, the pressure on the spring was released and there appeared suddenly in the accounting classroom a great white cloud, with Dr. Bob somewhere in the middle of it. After a few minutes, when the flour abated, there Dr. Bob stood, completely white from the shoulders up.

That's why I think of flour when I hear Dr. Bob's name mentioned. I always want to hum the Martha White Flour theme song.

I've always had a sense of camaraderie for Dr. Bob. We are both casualties of the same bomb squad.

An Embarrassing Way to Break Your Leg

One of my very best and richest friends is Bob Smith, founder and Chairman of Bob's Crafts, which hand-makes millions of beautiful hand-made crafts each year.

A customer who we'll call Laura reported that a broken leg was caused by one of Bob's crafts. As I understand it, here's what happened.

When the crafts arrived, Laura anxiously took them out of the box and admired them. Then something else reportedly came out the box that she did not admire, but which *did* make her more anxious:

A snake.

An alleged snake followed the crafts right out of the box. Laura screamed and ran, and when she returned, the snake did not. She knew he was somewhere, but the question was *where?*

Laura's husband, who we'll call Bobby, was thinking about that very question as he prepared for work the next morning. Being afraid of snakes, needless to say, he'd had a restless night. After checking the bathroom for any suspicious looking reptiles, Bob began to shave, with only a towel wrapped around his waist. It was at that moment that the family's large dog wandered in the bathroom behind Bob and stuck his nose under Bob's towel.

When Bob felt Spot's cold, wet nose, he did what any self-respecting, snake-fearing male would do. He fainted. Right on the bathroom tile. Knocked himself out.

His wife called the paramedics who loaded him on a stretcher and carried him out. As Laura opened the front door for them, the snake saw his escape opportunity and made a dash for the great outdoors. In so doing, he slithered between the two surprised paramedics, who dropped Bob, who broke his leg.

Babysitting with a Bone

One of the wildest conversations I've ever had occurred at church.

Bobby stopped me as I was walking down the hall. "Congratulations on the new addition to the family!"

This threw me at first. Brittney was almost a year old. Then it hit me. He was talking about Mike the Wonder Dog, our family's most recent addition. In retrospect, I should have clarified.

"So, where is she?"

"You mean he?"

"I thought it was - wait a minute - well, I guess you'd know."

"Thanks, Bobby. Yeah, I guess I would."

"Well, where is *he*?"

"Oh, Mike? He's at home."

"Oh, is he sick?"

"No, he's fine."

"Is Andrea sick?"

"No, she's here."

"Well, who's at home with Mike?"

"Precious."

"Is Precious a babysitter?"

"Precious is a dog."

Bobby was visibly shaken, unsure of what to say.

"You mean to tell me the only one home with Mike is your dog, Precious?"

"Yeah, Precious was glad to get a play mate."

"You let them *play* together?"

"Play together, sleep together and eat together."

Bobby was pale. He leaned against the wall, took out his handkerchief and wiped his forehead.

"I cannot *believe* you are saying this! Aren't you worried? I mean Mike is so young and you just - just - *left* him!"

"Calm down, Bobby. Mike is fine. As a matter of fact, I saw him as we were backing out of the driveway."

"You what?"

"Yeah, he was on his back with his legs up in the air. He was so cute."

I left Bobby standing against the wall. I thought I'd eased his mind when I said,

"Don't worry, Bobby. We tossed him a bone on our way out the drive."

The Williford
Christmas Tradition

The other night, the Williford family performed a time-honored Christmas tradition:

the toppling of the Christmas tree.

We chopped the tree, took it home, brought it in, put it in the new and improved stand, arranged the lights and ornaments and stepped back to admire it.

The tree was beautiful. We commented on how easy it had been. In years gone by, putting up the Christmas tree was a challenge. I would get it up and Andrea would want to move it. I'd move it to the new destination. It would lean. The stand would require readustment. Each readjustment required the readjuster - me - to crawl back under the tree, and in the process, acquire enough Christmas Tree needles down my shirt to mulch several flower beds.

Our tradition began the year our Dachshund, Pumpkin, decided to grab a dog bone biscuit ornament and make a dash for it. The ornament stayed firm, but not the tree. Pumpkin barely cleared the den before the crash.

Since that year, we've witnessed several spectacular falls. Every year I was determined to prevent another catastrophe. Every year, I was wrong.

On this most recent occurance, I was the crash culprit. After the tree was erected, decorated and perfected, I decided it needed a heavier restraining line. As I crawled under the tree to get to the small vacant space in the back corner, my back side pushed up one too many branches.

Down came the tree in one of the most spectacular of all our falls. Christmas lights popped before the cord was jerked from the wall. Ornaments cracked and exploded. Cedar needles rained over furniture and the carpet. The tree hit our brass lamp, jerking it out of the receptacle for a flash out of both ends of the lamp. As the tree settled over our many delicate Christmas ornaments, a sea of water was released by the new and improved Christmas tree stand.

I don't know if a tree makes noise in the woods if no one's around to hear it, but after years of research, I'm pretty sure it does in your den.

I just stood there. Andrea rushed in from the kitchen and then walked back out, muttering, "I *knew* it was too easy."

Brittney surveyed the damage, was certain I had ruined Christmas and rushed back to her room.

I was left with the tree. And the smoke. And the needles. And the water. And the ornaments. And the lights. None of which was where it should have been.

I wonder what my family would think about decorating the refrigerator this year?

That's Just the Way It Is

A friend of mine, Bill Linder, enjoys asking young children,

How come you're so good-looking and you're Daddy is so ugly?

I've heard him ask the question for years. The typical response he gets is:

"My Daddy is not ugly!"

Bill asked Brittney the question. She looked at Bill. Then she looked at me. Then she looked back at Bill and said:

"Well, that's just the way it is!"

A Haircut to Remember

One of the most humiliating experiences of my college
life happened when my girlfriend cut my hair.

As you may recall, during the '70s, we wore our hair
pretty long. I was not excited about Bobette cutting my
hair. She persisted. I gave in.

She told me to meet her in a classroom in the basement
of the Administration Building at David Lipscomb
College. She spread newspapers on the floor, put a
chair on top of the newspapers and produced scissors
and a comb.

So far, so good.

I sat.

She parted my hair in the middle and began working
on the left side. I hadn't seen it done like that before,
but I wasn't worried. She knew what she was doing.
She began to cut . . . and cut . . . and cut.

I began to sweat.

"How's it going?" I asked with as little panic as possible.

"Oh . . . fine. I didn't get it . . . even. I'm going to have
to cut a little more."

I looked at the newspaper. It held a lot of hair. What's worse, we - she was still on the left side.

She continued on that side for what seemed the rest of the school term. She began to mutter.

I hoped I didn't faint.

She sighed. "Let's move to the other side."

This did not sound good.

With the first cut of the right side, something else didn't sound good.

Ouch!

It was Bobette. She was holding her finger. It was bleeding.

I tried to look sympathetic. At the moment, I was more concerned about my hair. I hoped no one came in before she finished the right side. It would *certainly* be a strange sight.

Bobette wasn't cutting my hair anymore. She was still holding her finger. She went to the restroom. I sat waiting in the middle of the classroom, feeling like the world's goofiest college student.

When Bobette came back, she was had a paper towel wrapped around her finger. Her finger wouldn't quit bleeding. She tried to cut my hair with the paper towel on her finger. It didn't work. She took the paper towel off and began to cut . Finally, we were getting somewhere.

Then she began to sob. "I'm sorry. I can't do it."

"What do you *mean*, you can't do it?"

"I mean I can't cut your hair."

"What!"

"I'm sorry," she boo-hooed. "I'm getting blood all over your hair."

"Don't worry about my hair."

"And I'm getting hair in my cut."

"Don't worry about your - I mean . . . "

I felt panic. I was beginning to feel like a trapped animal. A very wierd looking, partially sheared trapped animal.

"Maybe somebody back at the dorm can finish it," Bobette sobbed. She put the comb and scissors in her purse.

"How am I supposed to *get* to the dorm?" I asked. "Do you expect me to walk across campus looking like this? And *who* in the dorm is going to cut my hair?"

"I don't *know*," she blurted. She picked up the newspaper with hair and blood on it and put it in the garbage can. "I'm so sorry. I have to go." She took one more look at my hair, burst into tears and left the room.

This was not good.

Alone, millions of miles from my dorm room, not knowing what to do next, it occurred to me that I hadn't seen what I looked like. I walked to the restroom. Fortunately, there were no classes going on in the basement. I flipped on the light switch and looked in the mirror, expecting the worst.

It was worse.

The right side of my hair was basically untouched. A shag hair cut that came over my ears and collar.

The left side of my hair was three to four inches shorter than the right side. Sometimes three, sometimes four. It was jagged. It looked like I got too close to a fan or vegematic.

I was horrified. I didn't want to go across campus looking like this. I would have traded everything I owned for a baseball cap. Thank goodness it was dark. I walked on the outer edge of the campus, ran to the dorm, ran down the hall and into our room

There were my friends, Jerry and Kim. They could help me. Jerry and Kim took one look at me and howled.

They fell out of their chairs and rolled around on the floor in convulsions.

I went over to the metal cabinet and slammed my hand on top of it as hard as I could. The noise exploded off the tile floor and concrete walls. It scared Jerry and Kim to death.

"I need help," I rasped. "Find somebody to cut my hair - *now!*"

Jerry and Kim left the room. Only later did I realize that they had no idea why I looked the way I did. In a few minutes, they showed up with a guy who claimed he had cut hair before. I'll never know for sure. He was kicked out later that term for having a machine gun under his bed.

I never let him cut my hair again, but he at least got both sides even. I found a baseball cap and a barber the next day.

I haven't talked to Bobette in almost 20 years. But I bet she remembers that night. To this day, Jerry and Kim can tell you exactly how I looked, what I said and how much they laughed when I wasn't around.

When you *really* embarrass yourself, nobody *ever* forgets!

A Split Second Embarrassment

Speaking of baptistries, a friend of mine, who I'll call Bob, is a preacher. A woman, Lillian, came forward during the invitation hymn and announced that she wanted to be baptized.

Bob talked to Lillian for a few moments and learned that the reason she hadn't been baptized before was her tremendous fear of the water. Especially going under water. But she felt like her desire to be baptized was stronger than her fear of the water.

Bob put on his hip boots and waded into the baptistry, which was about four feet deep. Lillian walked down into the baptistry, with Bob helping her.

The curtains opened to the congregation. Bob quoted a scripture, and announced he was now going to baptize Lillian.

He put one hand behind her back and the other hand on her shoulder. She had both hands clutching a handkerchief over her nose. Everything was fine.

It all happened so fast, Bob couldn't have expected it. In the split second before her face went under, Lillian screamed, *No!* and grabbed Bob's neck with one hand and his ear with the other.

The congregation, not being let in on Lillian's fear of water, was somewhat confused and fairly concerned as to just what was taking place in the baptistry.

Meanwhile, Bob was in a jam. He tried to pry her off, but Lillian was holding on to him like a lobster. Being a large, rather obese woman, she was also floating. Bob alternated between trying to get out of the vice grip and pushing the rest of her floating body under the water.

Finally, Bob made his decision, took a deep breath, and went under with sister Lillian holding on. They came up, gasping. Leaving the congregation to more or less do the same thing.

The Bee in
the Outhouse

We were spending the week with my grandparents in Saltillo, Tennessee. I was five years old. More importantly, I needed to go to the bathroom.

Occupied. Grand Daddy. Bad News.

No problem. I'll just go use the outhouse. After all, that's where we used to go, until they added the bathroom the year before.

I had always liked the outhouse, anyway. It reminded me of a barn. I liked the feeling of the wind coming through the cracks, hearing the birds sing and seeing blue sky through the roof. I also liked the feeling of independence an outhouse gave a five year old. Especially one that hadn't been used in a year.

It was a blissful experience until the bumble bee landed on my leg. I stared at him in horror. He had a message. He wanted me to know that he did not appreciate me sitting on his home, invading his nest, lowering the property value.

He stung me and flew away. I should have been thankful it wasn't several simultaneous messages. I wasn't. I was horrified. Stunned. Scared. In pain.

So I ran. I wanted distance between me and the
outhouse as quickly as possible. I did not take time for
such matters as pulling up my underwear or jeans.

That's how I appeared in Granny's kitchen. Panting,
sobbing, wearing my pants and underwear at ankle
height.

After everyone determined it was not a snake or
animal bite, calmed me down and advised me to steer
clear of the outhouse (unnecessary), they've seen fit to
remember this incident ever since.

An Unfortunate Serve

Bob was on the tennis team in college. He is a well-known athelete in Memphis. I had always wanted to play tennis with him. He called and asked me to be his partner in a doubles tournament. I was excited.

Of course I couldn't use my crummy racquet, so I borrowed a friend's. The grip was a little big for me, but it looked good.

Our warm-up was great. The new racquet delivered more power. We tied the first set and played a tie-breaker. We lost it, due to a couple of mistakes. Mine.

I could feel my hands getting sweaty. On my next service, I knew the pressure was on. I served as hard as I could and still keep the ball in. With the new racquet, I had more control, so I served harder. I hit what had to be an ace. But it was returned. A hard, low ball, deep to my backhand. I got in position, planted my feet and took a mighty swing. That's when the ill-fitting racquet left my sweaty hand. It soared high into the air. We watched it sail over the court next to ours and into the middle of the *next* court. It stopped play on all four courts.

Bob retrieved my racquet. I was mortified.

I took a towel and dried the grip and my hand. The pressure was on. I had to serve an ace or one that Bob could easily put away when returned. I held my racquet extra tight, I threw the ball in the air, I gave the ball an extra hard serve . . . and proceeded to hit Bob's posterier. The ball popped so loud, people three courts away yelled, "Ouch!"

Bob never took his eyes off me again when I served. He also never asked me to play doubles with him again.

But I think he still remembers our match.